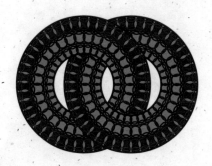

My

Crooked

House

My

Crooked

House

Teresa Carson

CavanKerry ❖ Press LTD.

CavanKerry Press Ltd.
Fort Lee, New Jersey
www.cavankerrypress.org

Publisher's Cataloging-in-Publication
(Provided by Quality Books, Inc.)

Carson, Teresa, 1954–
My crooked house / Teresa Carson.
pages cm
Poems.
ISBN 978-1-933880-43-3

I. Title.

PS3603.A7763M9 2014   811'.6
QBI14-600063

Cover photographs are used courtesy of the author
Cover and text design by Gregory Smith
First Edition 2014, Printed in the United States of America

My Crooked House is the tenth title of CavanKerry's Literature of Illness imprint. LaurelBooks are fine collections of poetry and prose that explore the many poignant issues associated with confronting serious physical and/or psychological illness.

CavanKerry Press is grateful for the support it receives from the New Jersey State Council on the Arts.

For my husband, John

ALSO BY TERESA CARSON

Elegy for the Floater (2008)

The Congress of Human Oddities: A Narrative of 19th Century America (2012)

Contents

Homeless

Home Away from Home

Homesick

Homework

Homemaking, Part I

Homemaking, Part II

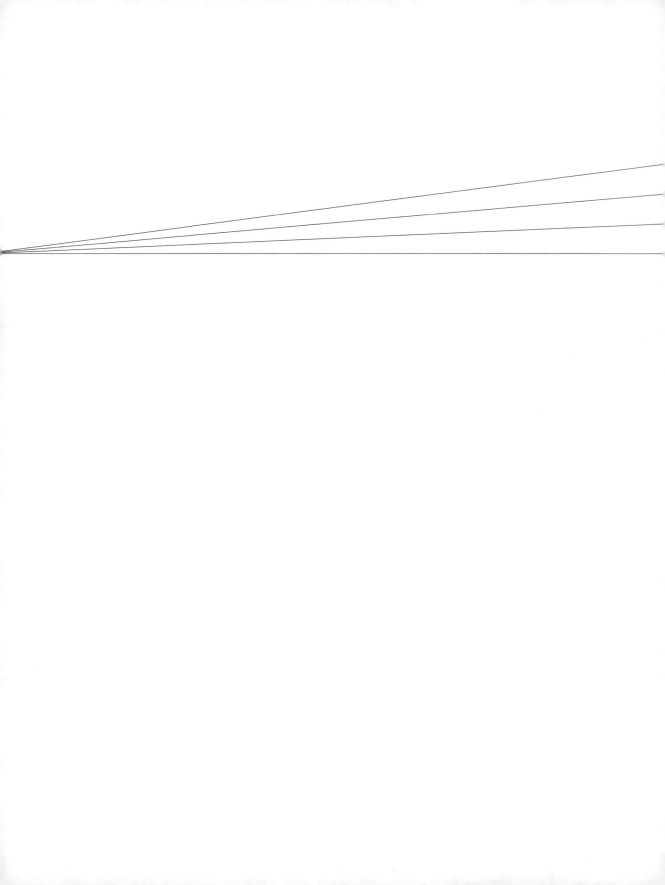

Foreword

Just what is it that leads someone to experience excruciating fear in circumstances that are completely safe? Why do some people check the door repeatedly when they know in their heart-of-hearts that it is already locked? How can someone believe wholeheartedly that their mission in life is to rescue cats, but then live with large numbers of them in squalid conditions that threaten the health and safety of themselves and the animals? I have spent a career studying these questions. But my views are constrained by the language of science and clinical practice. These lenses are myopic, limited by structures placed on them by a profession. The poets lens is not so constrained. It is rich with nuance that reveals a new world of information. There is the power in this work, power that transcends a scientific understanding.

These poems weave a tapestry of several lives, the life of a house, the life of a family, and the life of a poet. They also offer a template for resilience following a lifetime of suffering at the hands of a dysfunctional family and a destructive and manipulative psychiatrist. The author's house does not become a home until she does the thing she cannot bear. She must experience the pain she has avoided for so long. This lesson is clear for the rest of her life as well. She must embrace the fear to conquer her panic. She must relish in uncertainty to surmount her perfectionism. She must give up the responsibility of saving the cats of New Jersey. Bad things can happen; being perfect can't prevent them; collecting needy cats can't prevent them; avoiding anxiety can't prevent them. Bad things happen, but these poems are good things.

Randy Frost, Ph. D.

Harold Edward and Elsa Siipola Israel Professor of Psychology

Smith College

Co-author of *Stuff: Compulsive Hoarding and the Meaning of Things*

See how the light has come, and the hard curb
that held the house is broken!
Arise, O house, arise, too long you've lain
in shambles on the ground.

Aeschylus, *The Libation Bearers*
(translated by Alan Shapiro and Peter Burian)

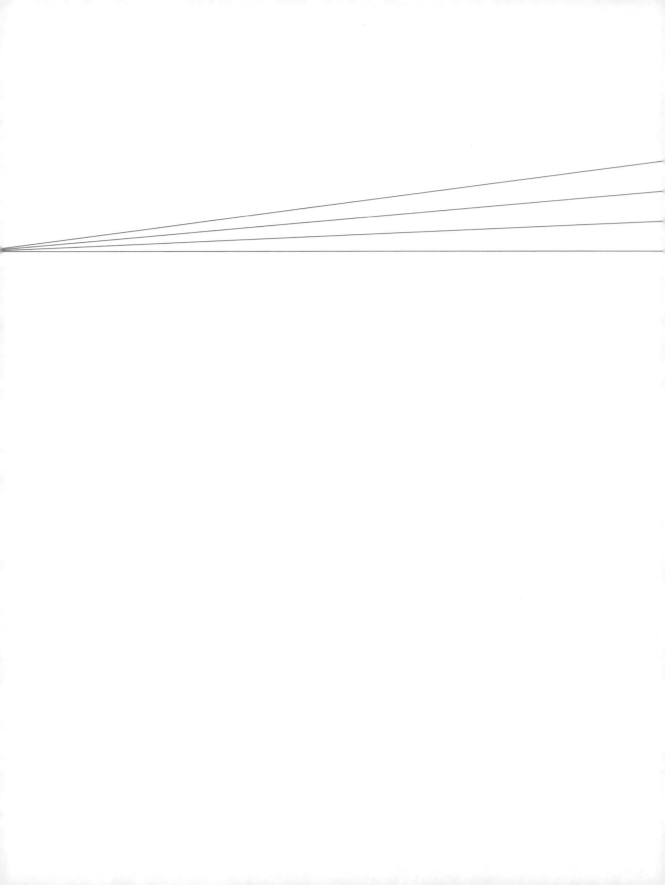

My

Crooked

House

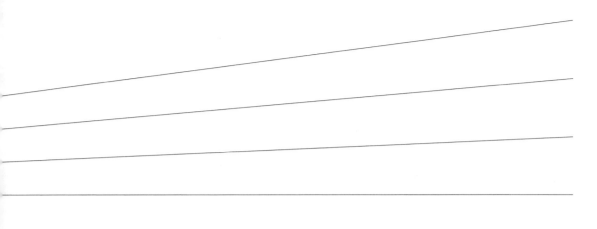

Concussion

First words I say: "Call 911."
First words John says: "Yes Yes."
Next words I say: "I'm really scared."
Next words John says: "Me too."

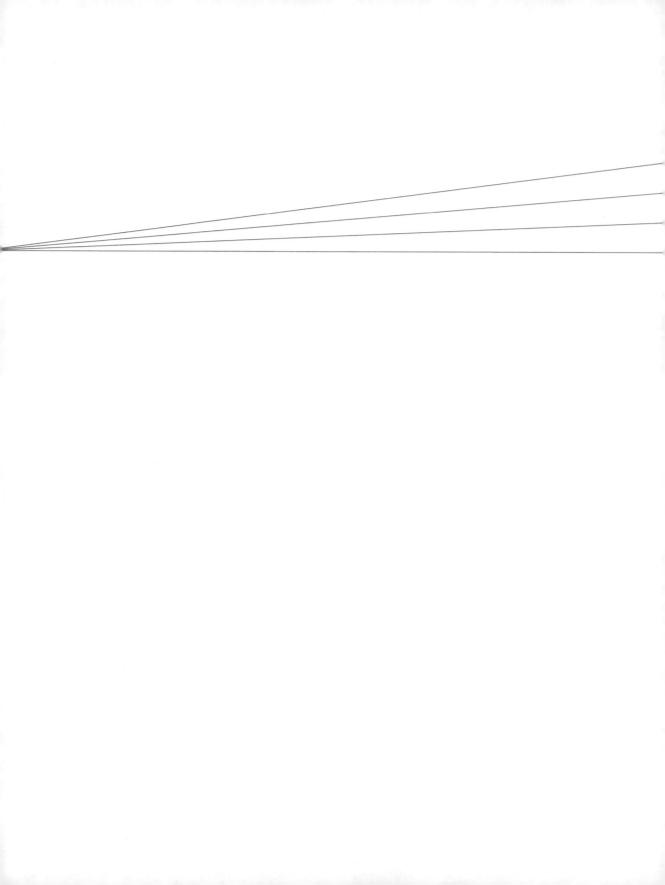

Homeless

How It Happened, Part 1

There's nothing special about her fifteenth pregnancy.
No warning signs prompt her to strike a deal
with Saint Teresa of Avila—
"I get a healthy baby; she gets your name—"
the way she did with the patron saint of mothers, Anne.

There's nothing special about her tenth delivery.
Despite the speed of my birth
she gets to East Orange General in time—
unlike what happened with Joe,
born in the back of a cab.

There's nothing special about me.
I look, feel, smell, eat, cry, and shit just like
all her previous newborns.
She doesn't even need to warm me in the oven
like blue-baby John.

There's nothing special about how she mothers me—
can't bear to let me out of her sight.
But, as it's been for almost twenty years,
she's pregnant with the next
before I toddle away.

There's nothing special about this.
She'll drop me
as soon as number eleven comes home—
the way she dropped Tom who had been, till I showed up,
the apple of her eye for forty months.

Except she has a miscarriage,
so bad it ends her childbearing days.
Suddenly I am special.
Suddenly I am "the baby of the family"
forever.

Pieces of My Father, Prologue

A man without a family history. No photos of his mixed in the box with those of my mother's family. No moments—letters, birthday cards, or diplomas—from his childhood. No gravesites visited on Palm Sunday. He didn't say much about what counties in Ireland his parents emigrated from or why they ended up on East 66th Street or how his supposedly impoverished father gave enough money to the parish of Saint Vincent Ferrer to warrant *Samuel Lamphier & Fmy* carved in the sanctuary wall. The closest we've ever come to touching young Samuel was finding his nine-year-old name on the 1920 census. His beginnings boil down to the often-told-by-Mom-tale of the dreadful consequences, after his saintly mother's death, of his father's marriage to a drunk who hated her stepson.

Me and Mom, 1961

It's her room,
not mine.
Her girly-pink walls, her jumble of junk,
her dirty sheers.
There's no drawer
for me.
I dig through a clump of underpants
to find a pair of mine.
My uniform's thrown on the chair,
topped by her girdle and slip.
The lit Virgin Mary centered on sill.
Polish can't save my saddle shoes.
Every night, when she goes to bed,
I must go, too.
Even if I'm reading
or playing tic-tac-toe or . . .
My mother's fat,
good thing I'm small.
Just one wool army blanket
to cover two. No pillows.
I press between her arm and breast.
What's that noise? And that?
I inhabit nightmares.
Her unwashed female stink takes over me.
I can't breathe.
No room to move.
Where else could I go?
Who else would hold me?
Don't want to.
It's all I've ever known.

Yes, my room,
not yours.
The only space that's mine, all mine.
Don't tell a soul.
My bureau,
not yours.
Why bother separating ours?
Stop wanting more.
This closet, those hangers, mine,
not yours.
Blessed art thou . . .
Don't press your luck.
I'm tired,
you must be, too.
(Yawn.)
Stop what you're doing.
My comfort matters most,
not yours.
(Lifts arm in invitation.)
Don't think you're better than me.
This is the way it always was.
This is the way it always should be.
Always will be.
Stop making up tall tales.
Mine,
not yours.
Yes.
Mine alone.
Everybody knows
you're mine.

Pieces of My Father 1

Who can blame him? One minute it's 1934 and, in this photo, he's the snazzy, dapper, twenty-three-year-old guy who has survived on his own since the age of fifteen when his father and stepmother threw him out on the streets of New York. Sure, he dropped out of high school but found work at Otis Elevator. He has big dreams—you can tell that from how his energetic smile stares straight at the camera, how his body relaxes yet perches, how he slightly separates himself from the others. He looks like the guy who spins a good yarn, who charms the ladies, who expects his lucky break in the not-so-distant future. Sure, he had a rough start but he's a fast learner, works hard, craves what money buys, worships in the church of "the self-made man." Like Dickens. Like Carnegie. Like him.

Broken Doors

Whose fist smashed the glass panel out of the front door to our apartment?
Pop? Most likely.
Mom? Less likely, but possible.
One of my brothers? Likely.
One of my sisters? Unlikely.

Who installed the cheap plywood panel, held in place with a few nails, which replaced
     the glass panel?
The fed-up-with-our-shenanigans super? Most likely.
My father? Unlikely.

Whose hand first slipped between the edge of the panel and the edge of the frame and
     turned the lock?
Someone without a key.
Why didn't Mom hear the knocking?
Asleep? Likely.

The door was always locked.
We had no keys.
We didn't bother to knock.
Our hands always slipped in and turned the lock.
Did Mom or Pop say a word about fixing it? Unlikely.

A stranger could have done the same.
It didn't take eagle's eyes to spot the opening.
And once he was in, he was in. Who would stop him?
Pop? He wasn't home too often.
Mom? Unlikely.

When it was down to Mom and me in that apartment I slept in a room near the front door.
Night after night I listened for the stranger's hands.
Would I die in those rooms with her?
Likely.

Pieces of My Father 2

Maybe marriage to my mother wasn't part of his original dream but they look happy enough in the early photos, especially in the ones with their first child. Then, in the blink of an eye, he's saddled with a toddler, a dead infant, and a wife who's so depressed she can't take care of their apartment, their son, or him. There's no one to help out. Somehow they struggle through and things start to look up; then, bam, their third child arrives and his wife has a complete breakdown. A few more blinks: now there are five more mouths to feed and she goes in and out of Pilgrim Hospital while the kids go in and out of orphanages but, finally after twelve years of shaky jobs, he lands a solid union job at Bendix—where he climbs the ladder as high as a dropout can—and catches his breath.

Herbie

On my seventh birthday, my sister-in-law gave a soft beaming hippo to me.
Though I'd owned a doll or two, nothing ever felt mine-all-mine until he was in my arms.
When we were apart, even for a second, I couldn't fully breathe.
Wherever he was, the ground was solid.

His presence kept the bleakness that chilled those rooms out of my heart.
He saved my heart.
Through him I believed there was something else.
Through him I believed someone could love me.

What made my brother Tommy hatch the plot? Neither he nor I recall—
maybe the sight of me releasing secrets into ever-attentive brown felt ears?
He kidnapped Herbie; scissored his ears, tongue, tail; stuffed him in the hamper of
        dirty clothes.
After frantic hours of loss, I rescued him.

Mom missed the mark: "Your brother wouldn't hurt a fly."
Tommy, pressed to her side, stuck out his tongue.
Pop had better things to worry about when he got home.
My other siblings pounced: "What do you have to cry about? You weren't sent, like we
        were, to the orphanage for years."

And me? Did I find a hiding place big enough for sweet disfigured Herbie and me?
No, I already knew there wasn't one.
No, while my face stared straight ahead, my hands did what they had to do:
shoved Herbie, head first, into the trash.

Pieces of My Father 3

He rents a place in Newark. Mom comes home for good. All the kids come home for good. The dust settles. Then, out of the blue, he's charged with manslaughter because he pushes the landlord, during a fight over said landlord's crude remarks to my mother, and the man falls backwards down the stoop, cracks his head, and dies. Though the charges are dropped, the man's family threatens revenge, which is why my family moves to Jersey City. Now it's 1954, twenty years after the photo of dreams, and he's stuck with a nutcase who he can't take out in public, a filthy home, which he can't bring friends into, and nine needy kids. This wasn't the way things were supposed to go. Now in every photo his fed-up face fumes, "For chrissakes, I deserve better than this." Yes, he does.

The Ice Skates

Every winter Jersey City opened an ice skating rink at Roosevelt Stadium; admission was free but it cost fifty cents to rent skates. My best friend had received white skates adorned with candy-stripe laces and white pom-poms for Christmas and wanted to use them. Whatever she wanted, I wanted too but I didn't have skates and my parents couldn't give the money to rent them. In the back of the deep hallway closet, where I often hid, was an unclaimed pair of men's hockey skates. I stuffed socks in the toes of those skates until they fit my feet. I polished the boots with white shoe polish until the black leather was covered with white, until they looked, if you didn't look too closely, like girl's skates.

We were twelve and had started to notice boys. Within minutes, my friend joined the stream of skaters gliding clockwise around the rink. Boys followed her, started doing spins, turns, and stops to catch her eye. After falling a few times, I stayed by the boards, stumbling this way and that in my toe-stuffed skates. Worst of all: the more my feet banged into the boards, the more the white polish wore off, exposing the shameful black boots, until it was all too obvious that my skates were not what they pretended to be.

Pieces of My Father 4

On Mondays, Wednesdays, and Fridays he wheels a shopping cart to the local A&P on Monticello Ave. Because I'm the baby of the family, he often takes me. Because he cashes his check on Friday, that's the day of the big shop—one that always includes canned spinach and might include Scooter pies. He plops me into the child seat and away we go, up and down the aisles. I love this part of the trip. When he gives a push then lets go, I laugh out loud. At the checkout counter I love that the store manager stops whatever he's doing to come over and chat with my father. The part I don't love happens when the cashier says, "That'll be XYZ dollars," and my father frowns, pulls items—the Scooter pies first—out of the order, and asks, "What if I get rid of them?" That question ruins the walk home, the rest of the night, and, really, my relationship overall with him until the day he dies.

My First List

May 19, 1967
Real Name: Teresa Anne Lamphier
Birthdate: October 4, 1954
Color "Hair": Brown
Color "Eyes": Brown
Parents' Names: Samuel and Joan
Sister's Names: Mary, Joan,
Ann, Louise
Brothers' Names: Vincent, Joseph,
John, Thomas
Instruments: Guitar and piano
Ambition: Train horses
Hobbies: Horses, sewing
Horses, writing,
Horses, reading
Horses, cooking
Horses, drawing
Likes: Horses,
smell of horse stables,
galloping on the beach
Favorite singer: ~~Davy Jones~~
Pete Seeger
Favorite drink: ~~Devil Shake~~
Wine
Likes: Ravi Shankar
incense, Indian culture

Can be found on pages 1 through 5
of this, my first diary which,
on the cover, beneath FRODO
LIVES, is titled, in emerald ink,
"THOUGHTS."
It's really a series of lists—
based on stock questions asked
of teen idols in *Tiger Beat*.
Written on top line: "Me";
Underneath that: All the Facts!!!
(Guitar and Piano? Huh?)
Although for my eyes only,
many of my answers weren't
true…not about the real me
anyway—e.g., my horse
obsession. After all, I'd been
near, not on, a live horse once.
But Davy Jones, my "Favorite
Singer," loved them which meant
I had to love them, too,
or he could never love me.
Six months later I changed some
answers to echo what my siblings
praised—Wine? Shankar?
These new "facts" were even less
true than what had been there before.

I WORK MY FINGERS TO THE BONE. *April 25, 1972 Dear Doctor Pollack*, It's always and forever about money with him. **I DON'T HAVE A POT TO PISS IN.** *Enclosed find check which is my final payment.* He throws away every last dime of his hard-earned pay on us. **DO YOU THINK MONEY GROWS ON TREES?** *My daughter Teresa is not old enough to incur debts for me.* He'd stop yelling if I could only stop wearing out the soles of shoes, leaving on lights, getting cavities, wanting Scooter Pies. **JESUS, MARY, AND JOSEPH! MORE?** *So in the future I don't want any bills charged to me without my written consent.* When I grow up, I'll understand. **I'M NOT MADE OF MONEY.** *Thanking you for your forbearance in the above debt.* Yes, I will.

The Search

During my childhood at 111 Belmont, I rummaged through messes in drawers and closets, on bookshelves and tables, under plates and the Infant of Prague. I examined old medical bills and stared at photos of my mother's family, whose stares I couldn't read.

After Mom kicked me out of hers, I jumped from one abandoned bedroom to the next, inheriting heaps of outgrown clothes; clip earrings from the 5&10; combs with teeth missing; orphaned books; limp school ties; broken-legged dressers with no mirrors.

Those relics stayed in place; I squeezed my box of belongings around and between. Never mattered much anyway what I did, or didn't do: no room would ever become mine when it continued to be called, even by me, *Mary's* or *the boys'* or *Mom's old room*.

I sifted through layers of remains in that apartment the way an archaeologist, not wanting to miss the smallest clue, sifts through dirt. Three times felt close: Mom's red pumps from the thirties; a hand-sewn christening gown; hoard of my report cards saved by Pop.

Time and again, I searched in the same spots, always waiting for the *big find*, which would tell me what I needed to know—though, at the time, I didn't know what that was.

Pieces of My Father 6

When I'm twelve he throws off the pretense of being a family man and starts going away whenever he gets a chance, which is often. He builds a second life with friends we don't know. A woman we don't know acts as his wife in this other life. He plays golf and goes to Florida in the winter in this other life. He eats in restaurants. Of course, he always does a big grocery shop before he goes away. And he leaves some money for us: ten dollars for a weekend trip, fifty for a week or more. That money has to cover all expenses for Mom, Johnny, Tommy, and me. Mom doesn't have any other money. Behind our backs, he tucks folded bucks under the pile of plates in the cupboard. Right after he leaves, I check how much so I can start counting the days until he comes back. If he comes back.

How to Fight Off Hungers

At first: under table when he explodes, on windowsill when her eyes blank.
(Fold up in corner of closet at chorus of slamming doors.)
The week in bed with chicken pox: drab woolen army blanket, wrinkled sheet,
her fringed chenille coverlet, thick with her smell.
(The line-dried sheet smelling of sky.)
As lower leg blisters from spaghetti water spill:
bite lip, offer up pain to God for sins.
(Think of next week, next month, next year, when twenty-one . . .)
But then: Broadway cast albums: *Funny Girl, Oliver!, West Side Story, Guys and Dolls.*
(Every word, every song. As if on stage.)
Gene Kelly or Fred Astaire?
(Astaire. No, Kelly. NO, definitely Astaire.)
Nancy Drew then Tolkien then Tolstoy then Eliot then Austen then Dostoevsky.
(Always another book to eat.)

Pieces of My Father 7

Every October the teacher calls me to her desk and tells me that my ten-dollar supplies fee hasn't been paid. The dentist only suggests braces for my crooked teeth because *his wife wants a mink*. At the free clinic, a student pulls my rotten eyetooth without paying attention to my screams. I hate invitations to pajama parties because my suitcase is a brown paper A&P bag. Every month, rather than ask for two dollars to buy sanitary napkins, I use a wad of facial tissues. I expect that when Mom buys clothes for me, even my uniform, my father will blow his top. I expect his refusal to buy a Christmas tree. I expect that before he returns from one of his longer vacations, we'll run through the folded bucks and that his first words will be complaints about our *goddamn wastefulness*.

About Time through Time, Parts 1–4

1. First Lessons

At the moment when I learn to tell time, I learn to distrust time. To stay in sync with the world, I know, as do my siblings (though we keep our *traps shut* and never ask why), to subtract, at first glance, fifteen minutes from the kitchen clock. It isn't the fault of the poor clock (there are many over the years); Mom sets the time fast and Pop leaves it that way when he moves the hands forward in spring, back in fall. I know this only happens inside our home—the time on any clock that isn't ours can be taken at face value. Still, the tried and true workaround fixes things until, out of the blue, five minutes get added. What seems under control isn't. From then on, I must keep an even closer watch on time.

2. Behindhand

Too late to have the Mom who smiled with all her heart at newborn Vin.
Too late to be a beatnik, like Mary, hitchhiking from East to West.
Too late to have the Pop who paid Joanie a buck to recite "The Wreck of the Hesperus"
      from memory.
Too late to know Joe before schizophrenia became him.
Too late to take two years of Latin in high school like Annie and Lu.
Too late to spend, like Johnny, the Summer of Love panhandling in the Haight.
Too late to have Tommy ever treat me as other than a threat.
Always too late for everything gone for good.

3. Salvation

One minute: sitting next to Mom on the couch.
On her lap: a yellow-bound *First Reader.*
She's much more alive than usual—what she's pointing out about the page must be why.
The next: a switch flips in my brain:
black marks become letters, letters combine into words, words have meanings,
meanings create different sets of rooms.
In the space between those minutes, my life with her becomes livable:
books will take me out of time for the time it takes to read them.

---

4. Early Time Jumping

I want to answer *ten*, not nine,
high school, not eighth grade.
I want to wear a bra, to have my period,
to be asked by a boy to go steady.
I want the first day of fall, not the first of summer,
1975 not '66.
I want whatever's happening this second in my life over with,
I want the end.

Pieces of My Father 8

Here's the funny part: despite the obvious contradictions between what he says and what he does, none of us questions his tale-of-woe about making barely enough to keep us out of the gutter. Mom doesn't ask how he manages to afford golf clubs and greens fees when he crabs about the cost of her false teeth. I don't ask how he manages to afford a *Hello, Dolly!* ticket when he crabs that my $200 high school tuition will bleed him dry. If we start asking questions he'll cut us off, slam the door in our faces, tell us never to set foot in his house again. Where could we go? Who else would put up with our crap? It's twenty-five years after his death before I dare to take a close look at 1040s—found in a box—from that time; now numbers, in his hand, prove what my child-heart knew then.

Near Death

The same man who raped me weeks ago picks me up at three.
I love him.
I'm wearing my school uniform—white blouse, navy weskit, navy pleated skirt,
       white knee-highs—and pink Keds.
He drives to Staten Island where people who owe him big bucks live.
They don't pay him; he steams because he owes to someone else.

He parks the van in the woods.
When he tries to stick his hand in my underpants I push him away.
"It's okay," he sweet-talks while slipping behind my back, *okay*.
His hands encircle my neck.
After the second it takes to catch on, I try to pry them off.
Last thought: I'll never be twenty-one.

I come to life with a scream.
Underpants past my knees.
He stops, acts as if nothing happened, drives to the ferry, dumps me.
I slump on the bench, turn from the cop who keeps looking my way.
For days, despite Indian summer heat, turtlenecks hide the necklace of bruise.
He drops out of sight. I cry over missing the chance to please him.

Pieces of My Father, Epilogue

Out on my own, I go to the supermarket on Friday, which is also payday for me. Despite the small number of items on my grocery list—e.g., dry cat food, breakfast cereal, one dozen eggs, frozen orange juice, tuna fish, cheese—I'm worried each and every time about coming up short on cash at checkout. Tallying the real prices doesn't help; I round up the price of each item to at least the next dollar and tally those prices in my head. Even then, as I place my groceries on the counter, heat rises in my face, my hands sweat and shake, my surroundings start to pull away, everyone's watching me, everyone's sneering at me, I don't think I can keep myself here, where's the door? Of course in all the years that I take care of me, not once do I have to say, "What if I get rid of them?" Not once.

Who and Would I Again?

Pepper—No
This list, written at sixteen, names the nine
Al—No
François—No
I'd had sex with in the eighteen months since
Scotty—No
Graeme—Maybe
the first name raped me. Didn't such a list
Billy—Yes
Johnny—Yes
show how grown-up I was? So what if while
Allen—No
Lance—Yes
they were fucking me, my self went somewhere else?

Home Away from Home

What Matters Most

I don't see myself in other girls.
I'm not cute like A, sweet-tempered like B, a spoiled princess like C,
poised, busty, chic, like her or her or . . .
Which means boys won't want me.
Which means I might as well be dead because that's what matters most.

I suck up to popular girls:
if they like me, and boys like them, boys will like me.
No. I end up as the drone, whose role is to flatter and fawn,
whose name is *friend of* _____,
who sits in the dark while inches away my best friend necks with a boy.

Then, at sixteen, when hanging out in Journal Square at 2 A.M.,
no other girls in sight—
their dads would kill them if they stayed out past midnight—
I stumble on an answer:
if I'm the only girl around, all of the boys will fall in love with me.

It takes work: I act *unlike* a girl—never mention cramps—
enough to pass for "one of them,"
yet *like* a girl—squeal at pigeons—enough to guarantee they never forget I'm not.
Sure, wearing two faces grows old fast;
but, in return, I get tons of what matters most.

How It Happened, Part 2

I enroll in Rutgers as a math major because it's the only program that accepts students who have graduated a year early from high school and, anyway, I've always been pretty good at math. But not at calculus: *rates of change* make no sense at all. A year and two majors later, I drop out mid-semester without having told a single soul that I, always a gold-star student with so little effort, am struggling to make *C*s. When my sisters realize what I've done, they call a family meeting: Get a job or find some place else to live.

Since fourteen I've had pocket-money jobs but don't know where to begin looking for one to support myself. At an interview for a job with punch-card computers, I'm doing really well until, in answer to a question about mental illness, I tell about seeing the psychiatrist when I was going through the court case with my parents because the judge wanted an evaluation of my mental state—to check if I had suicidal tendencies, which I didn't. The interviewer suggests reapplying in a year. When I go for a job as a lab assistant in a chemical plant, the owner says he doesn't hire girls for lab jobs and what a shame I don't type 60 words per minute or take shorthand because he likes my spunk.

My search flounders until I think of the phone company where my sister worked as an operator one summer and said the job was mindless but easy—yeah, it's beneath me but then who's kidding who? It's starting to look like I'm destined to be a blue-collar drudge, like Pop, for life. What I don't know when I walk into the N.J. Bell employment office is that the Bell System has just lost an Equal Employment Opportunity suit brought against it by female employees and has agreed to open up the better-paying, more prestigious, traditionally men-only "craft" jobs to all applicants. What I don't know is that, because of my score on the basic aptitude test, I'm given the advanced test for entry-level craft jobs.

They offer me a job as a "frameman," which pays twice what "operator" does. That fact alone is enough to make me say yes but they make me sit through a film in which middle-aged men, dressed in slacks and button-down shirts, take service orders from a bin and then proceed to connect or disconnect the mainframe wiring to fulfill that service order. None of them seems to be breaking a sweat. No, I don't mind working with all men. No, I don't mind working shifts. No, I don't mind getting dirty. Yes, yes, yes, I'll take the job.

"a man's, not a girl's, environment"

That's the trump card my first boss, a kind soul,
plays to explain why things are the way they are—
the use of *fuck* or *shit* as every part of speech,
the size-of-penis jokes, the let-loose farts, and Miss (fill in the month)
taped to the breakroom wall—and why warnings from HQ about
"complying with EEOC" do much more harm than good:
the troops refuse to yield an inch of "way it's always been"
to a "quota" who is stealing bread out of the mouths of some guy's wife and kids.
Their outrage overlooks the fact that most of them
have neither wives nor kids—most still have not left home—
what they really have are bar tabs and loans on 'Vettes.
Yet I bite my tongue about their faulty reasoning,
since nothing has proved truer than:
the Golden Rule for fitting in is "never disagree."

Panic Attacks

Once an episode starts, there's no turning back;
panic breaks out of the locked room in my gut, pushes sound thinking to the floor,
        then hungrily rampages through body and mind—
kicking aside anything in its way, taking delight in dangling me over the void—
until it has had enough fun for one day and lets go.
How have those full-blown attacks been kept to the min?
I'm crackerjack at spotting signs of trouble a mile off, sharp about running
        from an approaching twister.
What happens when early warning systems fail?
I pull the last-resort trick (useful in nightmares when that same old intruder shows up
        in my hallway in the dead of night) out of my sleeve:
shrink my self to the verge of not-even-there, take as few shallow breaths as possible,
pray she'll fail to notice me.
Sometimes that works.

Workplace Humor

When Jeanie left the breakroom—in a huff—
and Ernie humped the table edge which, seconds
earlier, her ass had pressed against,
I laughed along with all the guys.
When Harvey licked the breasts of Miss July,
then smacked, *Dem tits be finger lickin' good,*
I laughed so hard I nearly peed.
When Joe, our local's president, to strike
a blow against New Jersey Bell, branded
its CEO "a pussy," then—because
he noticed me—explained, "Don't get me wrong,
I love pussy but I don't want to be
one—*grin*—just fuck as many as I can,"
I laughed and laughed until my sides were split.

Why I Loved the "Bell System Practices"

There was no room for human error. Every detail of every task of every job title in every department in Ma Bell was spelled out in this library of 35,000 nine-digit documents.

There was no room for inconsistency. A switchman in Topeka and me, in Union City, both went to BSP 231-036-000 for the layout of the fuse panel on a Miscellaneous Frame.

There was no room for missing the mark. If my wire wraps looked exactly like Figure 4.2.8, then they were up to snuff and my boss would check "Meets All" on my evaluation.

There was no room for disorder. The health and robustness of the telephone network depended on the completion of hourly, daily, monthly, annual, and "as required" routines.

There was no room for uncertainty. Actions A, B, and C led to result D. Therefore, if you just performed the actions in the correct order, then any problem would be fixed. Period.

There was no room for argument. If actions A, B, and C didn't lead to D, then either you had screwed up or you were a screw up. (I mean, a chimp could follow these directions.)

There was no room for exceptions. Specially qualified men had determined the right way to do this or that. What a relief: *the* answer, in black and white, always at my fingertips!

Signs of Sophistication and Success List (Circa 1980)

1. Burberry trench coat
2. ~~Loden coat~~—I have my cashmere coat
3. Well-worn expensive leather briefcase
4. Signature fragrance
5. Flattering makeup
6. Manicured nails
7. Manicured toenails
8. Few pieces of clothing but good quality and matching
9. Housekeeper
10. Shelf filled with my publications
11. Dinner parties
12. Decorating house with a theme or interest
13. Diamond ring
14. Un-hurriedness about time
15. Original artwork collection—I've started collecting!
16. Pashmina shawl
17. Speak foreign language
18. Be asked to participate in readings
19. Acceptance by good journals
20. Ability to ask for what I want
21. Sense of my own style
22. Determined dedication to my writing
23. My red notebook
24. Fountain pen's sense of unhurried writing
25. <u>Knowing</u> Shakespeare's works
26. Wearing scarves every day

5. My Bedroom Clock

After leaving home, I copy, on every clock of mine, Mom's fifteen minutes fast; then, when I start working at the phone company, that becomes twenty; then, when my marriage breaks up, twenty-five; and finally, when the cats on the first floor become too many to take care of, half an hour. Doubts about the accuracy of the clocks and fear of forgetting what number to subtract become my constant companions. After John moves in, the clocks, one by one, get reset . . . except for the digital dual alarm on my side of the bed, which I change but, before the day is out, move forward again. Years pass before I let that last clock tell the right time at all times. Even longer before my heart follows suit.

6. On the Dot

Eight o'clock start means be on the floor at 0800 hours not at 8:04.
A record of any instance of tardiness will be kept in your personnel file. Your pay can be docked for tardiness of point one—i.e., six minutes—or more.
A fifteen-minute break means leave the floor at 0900 hours, not 8:58, and return at 9:15, not 9:18, certainly not 9:20.
Thirty minutes for lunch at 1630 hours means Lee's Tavern for quick burger and beer, then back running wires at 5.
Six minutes to run a new connect from line equipment in Union 4 to the 1920 cable, pair 164—a run of the block-long frame—means you take six, not five or seven, minutes and you better clean the old solder from the lugs and number-check your work.
Customer 5-codes have to be fixed within one hour while 4-codes can take a day.
During the first and last weeks of the month, the service order in-bin must be checked at 0700, 1300, 1600, and 1900 hours.
Five o'clock quit means leave the floor at 1700 hours, not at 4:55.

Annotated Map of Panic Attacks, Location A

#123 bus, inside Lincoln Tunnel, right past the N.Y./N.J. stripe.
Heat too high. Windows fogged over. Shuffling, unbuttoning coats, ripple of complaints.
Girl on cellphone: *Stuck in the tunnel.* Which we are. Which, since 9/11, never feels like just
an inconvenience. The bus moves west in fits and starts. Most of the passengers nod off,
check e-mail, or play video games. But the guy across the way stares at me. Why?
What did I show him by mistake? Turn head, but too late. Burn rises from chest to face.
Not now, not <u>now</u>. Must make the driver let me off, then run till I reach outside. Stop:
focus on white tiles, focus on blare from neighbor's earphones, focus on not going crazy.

Lunchtime at the Carousel

Most morning breaks are spent deciding where to go for lunch even though we usually end up following the routine—e.g., pizza on Wednesdays and Lee's Tavern, after cashing our checks, on Fridays—but when a go-go bar opens within walking distance, the guys always want to go there. I'm stuck having lunch alone. Worse, for the rest of the afternoon, they talk about the dancers: how Trish has the hots for this one or that; how, when Crystal bends over, her best assets show; what an asshole Lil' One's ex-husband is for leaving her and the kid. Suddenly I'm no longer the only woman in the room from eight to five, which means losing the amount, and kind, of attention that I crave. So,

I follow them to the Carousel where three bikini-clad dancers—around my age, to my surprise—stop chatting and start the show. I study NFL posters, then act as if lost in thought. The music flips between bump & grind and shake-shake-shake. The whooping guys, waving folded ones, reach around me. The dancers say "thanks" and "thanks." Back at work, when I open the attack on my rivals (her witchy eyeliner, her too-teased hair, her falsies, their lack of brains), my stomach cramps with shame—mine and theirs.

Chasing an Intermittent Trouble

There's an old intermittent trouble in the CC, the main memory, of the 1AESS switch in the Union City CO. Without warning it rears its ugly head and throws the system into a Phase 4. If you're standing in the equipment room, you hear every relay in the office drop. In a snap, 60,000 lines lose dialtone. In-progress conversations go dead. Alarms gong. Incoming/outgoing call attempts fail. Red lights start blinking all over the MCC.

Within seconds Tier-1 support in the local Switching Control Center calls Tier-2 support in the Electronic Switching Assistance Center. That's the group I'm in. Throughout the phone company world ESAC is considered an elite job; each of us has been handpicked to provide topnotch technical support in a specific technology. We're the "go to" people. We joke about "the few, the proud, the ESACers." Everyone expects miracles from us.

I don't feel elite. Most of the time I feel incompetent and inadequate in the face of the stomach-churning troubles that are thrown at us. Sometimes I, in the middle of yet another Friday at 4 P.M. crisis, go to the Ladies Room, cry, and repeat my mantra: anything broken can be fixed. The cherry on my anxiety: my male co-workers know the schematic diagrams by heart and can mentally trace the physical paths of calls. Not me.

Troubleshooting an intermittent trouble is akin to chasing a ghost through the machine. The usual bag of tried and true fixes never works. You have to dig deep inside the circuitry to find the faulty solder connection or the millimeter of exposed wire; but, finally, the equipment passes diagnostics so you close the ticket and everyone gives you a back pat. You're rid of it until, bam, that same damn trouble, or its first cousin, flares up.

Now, because Union City is my home central office, I'm stuck with this stinker. Though I manage to quiet it down for periods of time, I'm always on edge, waiting for its reappearance. It never lets me down. At the height of our battle, I order what amounts to a mechanical exorcism: the replacing of the wrapped-wire backplane. Yes, an extreme measure, but one that, without the shadow of a doubt, will vanquish the trouble for good.

For months, the longest time ever, the CC hums along without a hiccup. I, feeling vindicated, want to shout to the world, "See, I fixed what nobody else could fix. I really do belong in this elite group." Then ESAC gets the call: the failure has come back with a vengeance. The office has crashed in a fit of rolling emergency actions. My co-workers who have memorized the schematics step in and help me to restore sanity to the switch.

For my remaining two years in ESAC, I continue to wrestle with this trouble, though I've lost faith in ever fixing it. When the CC passes diagnostics, I simply push the ticket to the side of my desk in anticipation of the next time. When I move to another job, the trouble is still there. Years later, the Union City CO cuts over to the new 5ESS system; on the night they kill the 1AESS, the intermittent trouble in its main memory finally dies, too.

Homesick

Dr. Wright, My First Therapist, Evaluates Me

"Chance plays no part in birth:
souls pick their bodies, thus their destinies.
Your rotten soul picked out a rotten form
with which to lead your rotten life.
There isn't much that I can do
to fix a soul like yours, and if I can't,
then no one in the whole world can.
You might as well be dead."

Synonyms for "Make a List"

~~Cut~~ (no, someone may ask) <u>break</u> skin on arm, or thigh, by digging in with fingernails.

Follow, to a T, whomever you're, this minute, worshipping.

Lie, "I'm not hungry now," whenever offered food.

Obsess over why a friend did what she did because what she did wasn't nice.

Obsess over why a non-friend doesn't want to be a friend because if she doesn't want
        to be your friend, maybe there's something wrong with you.

Hurl plunger at the wall when cat hair clog won't budge.

Narrow daily food choices: oatmeal, tuna-fish salad on wheat, canned ravioli.

Show up ~~on dot~~ (not good enough) <u>early</u> for all appointments.

Schedule the same sex at the same time every Sunday.

Don't allow certain foods to touch on your plate.

Check, probably three times is enough, that you really did lock the front door.

Always offer to drive because you trust no one.

Don't wear brand-new, packaged-in-plastic socks until you wash them.

Consider becoming Episcopalian, Hindu, Unitarian, Sufi, or Buddhist.

Typical Journal Entry during Those Years

I never know what to do when she falls asleep.

This morning, thirty then forty-five then sixty then eight-five minutes passed.

I whispered, "Please wake up . . . twenty-five after seven . . . I must leave."

She, her eyes closed, snarled, "Why?"

"To go to work."

She asked, "You wasted my time by letting me sleep? Why did you let me sleep?"

I gave the expected answer, "To manipulate you into listening to my lies."

I'm not sure that was the truth.

I really don't know why I let her sleep but she'd explode if I said that.

She changed my time because my 6 A.M. sessions were "dangerous" to her well-being.

As she let me out of the building, she warned, "If you don't straighten up, I'll drop you.

Without me you'll end up in the gutter where beady-eyed lowlifes

like you and your mother belong."

I HATE HER SOMETIMES. I need her help. I still hate her.

Annotated Map of Panic Attacks, Location B

Ninth Avenue between Forty-Fourth and Forty-Fifth Streets.
Thursday, mid-afternoon, tree buds bursting. En route to my therapist. Without warning, the opening note: the disconnect from what's around me, as if my mind is falling backwards, out of reality. How can this be? An attack has never jumped me on a city street; in fact, that's where I feel safest. But here I am, in the middle of a sidewalk in Hell's Kitchen and the usual demonic notes (pounding, sweating, fleeing) tumble over each other to steal me from me. No one must know or see. I press into a doorway, wait for heartbeat to slow, for breath to ease, for voice in head screaming DEATH to shut up.

How It Happened, Part 3

At eighteen I move into my first	Rainbow
apartment; everything I own packed	Moonshadow
in four cardboard boxes. I furnish	Silver Boy
the two rooms with twin bed, chair,	
table. My neighbor's cat has kittens;	
I take two. My sister finds a Siamese	
in her yard but can't keep him; I can.	
By twenty I move three more times but	
the number of boxes stays the same.	
At twenty-one I marry. We buy	Raccoon
this house. His sister—divorced, two kids,	Binky
no job, lots of noise—moves into our	Eeeper
first floor. What had begun to feel like	
mine no longer does. I start therapy	
with Dr. Wright, who owns hundreds of cats.	
Maybe if I show how much I love cats,	
then she'll stop calling me *piece of shit*.	
Twice a day I feed strays in the yard.	
I'm thirty when that marriage ends.	Greystone
He kicks his sister out then offers,	Gawain
"If you want, you can live downstairs."	Harry
Not really, but Dr. Wright says it's	Ariel
the best choice for me so I agree.	Conan
My family praises how we're handling	Angel
the divorce. I discover my gift	William
for nursing the most hopeless cases.	Lily
Once they're inside, I don't let them leave.	Coco One
But this is still my fresh start, right?	Rose
Now I can control what happens, right?	Roscoe
I buy a queen-size bed, a white couch,	Blossom
three bookcases, an antique dresser.	Firecracker
After the cats, with claws and pee, make	Moonbeam

the mattress theirs, I sleep on the couch—
their warmth next to, on top of, between.
I bring home a date who leaves
quickly. When asked, "How many?" I lie.

My ex-husband moves out and moves on.
Dr. Wright dies. I move upstairs, leave
the cats downstairs. I buy a table,
a bed, a couch. Otherwise my rooms
are bare, as if nobody lives here.
My siblings see but don't say a word.
Nor do I. But there's no time to talk
anyway because there are always
starving, sick, or injured cats around.

And if I don't rescue them, who will?

Scooter
Buttons
Comet
Violet

Goldie
Hector
Helen
Oreo
Coco Two
Adder
Bart
Peanut
Donut

My Father's Back

After five years, his cancer returns.
The surgeon closes him up, says, "A matter of time."
He spends half of September, the whole of October in Christ Hospital.
He stops eating because he's had enough.
His room has a view of his much-loved Manhattan.
He won't get out of bed to look.
He wants me to rub cream on his sore back.
I want to do whatever pleases him.
I'm dying to show, once and for all, his baby's a good girl.
That way, when he leaves, I won't be left behind.
I've waited and waited for him to take me.
This is my best chance, my last.
But when he turns and reveals his yellow-tinged back,
I can't make my hand touch his skin.

Annotated Map of Panic Attacks, Location C

Yankee Stadium, terrace level, between third and home.
I don't like baseball but John's son bought tickets for us. By the time we reach the ballpark, I'm drained because I spent the ferry ride worrying if the orange vest under the seat would really save my life. Thought <u>that</u> was my hit of dark for the day until, in the second inning, when we stand up to cheer a great catch by the right fielder, the urge to throw myself over the railing overwhelms me. I lie to John: sun's too strong; need shade. Takes full attention to climb steep stairs without falling backwards. Halfway: rubbery legs. Drop to hands and knees? Crawl? Ask for help? No, keep going, just keep going.

Secrets to Keep

My sister glances around the first floor of my house and warns, "Don't tell anyone; they'll think you're crazy." What I must keep secret are the twenty cats that live in these four rooms and the dozen or more cats that come to my yard for water and food in clean bowls, shelter in cardboard boxes. What I must keep secret are piss-stained walls, windows, and book spines; claw-shredded couch and mattress; shit on top of kitchen cabinets and buried in flowerbeds; sour stench that I don't even smell anymore; claw gouges on door frames and antique dresser; fur and vomit and dirt and blood everywhere. I must keep it secret that I spend most of my salary on the cats; therefore, my house is barely furnished, needed repairs get put off, and the fridge doesn't hold much more than coffee beans and a quart of milk. I make a good living but live on the verge of broke. Yet I can't stop picking up strays, can't stop letting them take over my life. What I must keep secret is how I am, in my home, just like my mother. I must keep these secrets because no one must ever think of me as "crazy"; everyone must think of me as "normal," "nice," "neat." Furthermore, I must never forget what others think of me will affect what they think of my sister. I must keep all these secrets not only to protect me but also her because she doesn't want, God forbid, anyone to think she might be keeping secrets, too.

Suggested Schedule for January 3–8, 1988

Sunday
    ★★Make note of 2 behaviors during day—jot down situation and how I behaved★★

11:00 A.M.–1:00 P.M.	Tai chi
1:00 P.M.–6:00 P.M.	Go for walk with A & P or by self or go to movie or exhibit
6:00 P.M.–bedtime	1. Iron clothes for week
	2. Start first book on reading list
	3. Write in diary
	4. Review notes on behavior

Monday
    ★★Make note of 2 behaviors during day—jot down situation and how I behaved★★

5:00 A.M.	Wake, shower, feed cats & birds
6:00 A.M.–7:00 A.M.	Write
7:00 A.M.	Breakfast, dress, do Dr. Wright exercises
8:00 A.M.–5:00 P.M.	Work
	1. Read one article in newspaper and evaluate it in terms of Dr. Wright information
	2. Find info in BSP on 1AESS translations and use
	3. Walk at lunchtime
	4. Vocabulary—study 3 words
5:30 P.M.–8:30 P.M.	Work OT
	OR
	1. Make index card for each cat
	2. Begin to read background for first book on reading list
	3. Do Tai chi form 3X
	4. Diary
	5. Review behavior notes
	If working OT do only 3, 4, 5

Tuesday

Make note of 2 behaviors during day—jot down situation and how I behaved

6:00 A.M.–10:00 A.M.	Same as Monday
10:00 A.M.	Dentist
	If time before work: continue reading first book on list; walk; dry cleaners
1:00 P.M.–9:00 P.M.	Work
	Same as Monday (items 1, 2, 3)
After work–bedtime	Same as Monday (items 3, 4, 5)

Wednesday

Make note of 2 behaviors during day—jot down situation and how I behaved

5:00 A.M.–5:00 P.M.	Same as Monday
6:00 P.M.	Cat to vet
Night	1. Hockey game
	2. Begin reading nutrition info
	3. Pick one book and start to read
	4. Same as Monday (items 3, 4, 5)

Thursday

Make note of 2 behaviors during day—jot down situation and how I behaved

5:00 A.M.–noon	Same as Monday
Afternoon	Visit with Joan
Night	Same as Monday (items 3, 4, 5)

Friday

Make note of 2 behaviors during day—jot down situation and how I behaved

5:00 A.M.–5 P.M.	Same as Monday
6:00 P.M.–8:00 P.M.	Swimming
8:00 P.M.–bedtime	Go to movie
	OR
	Same as Monday (items 3, 4, 5)

The Last Session

Though I return from a business trip in plenty of time to make that therapy session,

When the cops respond to "complaints of foul odors emanating from the building," they find Dr. Wright in her bed.

I don't go.

She has been dead for "several days." Natural causes.

Early next morning, as if eager, I call to reschedule.

But her corpse isn't the main source of the stink.

The phone rings and rings—as usual—and I, arming myself against the inevitable accusation about my spiteful habit of not giving her enough time to answer, let it ring until the phone company disconnects the call with: "the party is unavailable."

They find "cats, hundreds of them, living and dead, interspersed amid mountains of debris."

How many days, how many dozens of calls, how many cycles of dread/relief before a stranger picks up, "What do you want with Dr. Wright?"

They remove her, remove the dead cats, capture as many live cats as they can, chain the front door, and leave.

I over-explain my desire to reschedule a session that, unfortunately, was missed because of a very important out-of-town . . .

Three years later, the building is sold. Cleanup workers find, amidst seven floors of debris, 500 more cats—all dead, all rotting.

The stranger cuts short my story with the news.

"No matter what they do," the real estate broker says, "the smell of death has become part of that place."

Homework

Re-siding

The house slumps as if its frame doesn't have enough strength to withstand the chaos inside. Pieces of faded blue siding break off and leave jagged edges behind. Its windows are sunken eyes. The white paint on the proud, carved cornice peels, exposing tired wood. Town drunks lounge away afternoons on the stoop, snore overnight in the weed-thick front yard. I don't look at the house when approaching it, when climbing the steps, when unlocking the door. I live in it but won't look at it. As if I don't care a whit. As if I've got more important things to think about. As if you can't tell a book from its cover. As if the shape of the face doesn't tell the whole, the real story. As if it has nothing to do with me.

Two years into our marriage, John suggests re-siding. I stand perfectly still, though my heart runs away, while a stranger pries, pokes, and makes a list of "what has to be fixed or else." John holds my hand. We pick stucco over vinyl. We pick subdued: grey, black, and white. We pick keystone moldings for windows. Every choice feels life or death.

The workers speak Spanish; I don't. Yet I'm sure they're joking non-stop about the insane number of cats inside and out. I'm sure they're criticizing the rundown condition of my life in general, the disgusting condition of the first floor in particular. I'm sure they hold their noses at the cat stink that I no longer smell. I'm sure they hate showing up here each day. I'm grateful they show up at all. I bet they've never seen anything as bad as this in their lives and that they never want to again. I'm sorry they have to work on such a damaged house. I'm sure they'll do a half-assed job because it doesn't deserve to be treated any better than that. I'm sure they'd love working on the house if it were perfect.

The foreman says, "Hello," to me but little else. Whenever he needs an answer, even if I'm in right in front of him, he seeks out John. I'm sure he blames me for the décor of dirty, neglected, and wrong. I'm sure he wouldn't give the time of day to the kind of woman who'd let her house get this out of control. I'm sure he wonders why nice-guy John doesn't dump me for something better.

Every morning, while the world pauses between dark and light, I fill the food bowls for the outside cats. Before long, a whiff of the unfamiliar sends the cats scurrying to other yards. I can't protect them. A laughing worker wings a rock at a young tabby that dares to wander back. I warn the inside cats to stay out of sight because I won't be able to protect them if something bad happens. Every evening, as soon as the last worker leaves, I rush out and, while filling the bowls with more food, apologize to the returning cats. The minute the job begins, I want it over with. I hate the house for putting us in danger. The house that I've always dreamed about living in would never need any work done on it. When the workers start tearing off the siding, I turn the lights off and hide in our bedroom. I can't bear the sounds of skin being ripped from the body. I can't protect the house. I can't bear the signs of longstanding sickness—cracked siding, twisted flashing, rusty nails—lying in the open. I shy away from looking at what was waiting underneath.

When the top layers are gone, John and I examine what's left: the original one-inch-thick wood sheathing, the bluestone foundation. He praises the sturdiness of its four-by-eight basement beams. I hear him but wish the house were made of brick. While it was built in the same period —about one hundred years ago—as my sister's brownstone and our friend's rambling Victorian, it doesn't possess their charm. No one in my family ever says, "Teresa, you're so lucky. I wish this house belonged to me." And it has scars: on the north side, above the window in the second-floor bathroom, the workers exposed a charred patch from an old fire that did damage, yes, but couldn't burn it to the ground.

The house may have good bones but it's vulnerable and I can't love it. The house may have lots of stories to tell but it's plain and I can't love it. The house may wear its scars well but it's imperfect and I can't love it. The house may belong to me but I can't love it. I can't get past the fact that this house was never, is not, will never be, the house I want.

The second stage of the job—the application of the new facade—is no less painful. I flinch when the workers' callous hands touch the naked sheathing. I want to run out and push those hands away. I want them to leave us alone. I want to put my arms around the violated house. I want the cats to come out of their hiding places. I want to turn on the lights. I want to change my mind, to let things go back to the way they were, to stop trying so hard. The job drags on for two weeks; then, finally, they clean up. The next morning, John and I look at the results from across the street, from the yard, the alley. As we look closer and closer, I see the unexpected: this house becoming a, no, *our*, home.

Annotated Map of Panic Attacks, Location D

New Jersey Turnpike, Mile 108.8.

Regular route home from work. On the bridge over the Passaic River, the very bridge from which my brother may have jumped. As the road rises and curves, the cement mixer in front drops below speed limit. Pull into middle lane; end up behind a car-carrying trailer. Can't keep my eyes off its last dangling car. Can't help wondering how secure those chains are. Pull into outside lane to pass. Except now we're going downhill, he picks up speed, we're side by side, pushing eighty, there's an SUV on my ass, no way to get out of the way, then something inside urges me to jerk the wheel, send car careening into concrete divider or semi's tires. White-knuckle steering till I break free.

Cleaning the First-Floor Bathroom

When a room has been abandoned for

After plunging the blocked tub, a whispered, strangled sound.
John snakes out clumps of fur and plaster chunks.
Water rushes through pipes.

as long as this one has, it takes a lot

The layer of scum that lines the sink easily wiped with sponge.
Plenty of claws were sharpened on the vanity's veneer—
nothing can hide the damage there.

of time, of work, of strength, to clean the mess,

The inside of the toilet bowl hasn't been cleaned in years—
why bother when no one, just cats, lived here?
The oldest stains refuse to budge no matter how I scrub.

and traces of the damage stay for life.

No Doorbell

Despite CARRIER LEAVE IF NO RESPONSE on the address label, the carrier did not do what he was told but, instead, left a beige slip that let me know the package would be available for pickup the next day after 9 A.M. at the branch post office three blocks away.

Scrawled on the slip his reason for not leaving it: NO DOORBELL. Our regular carrier—who would have just tucked it between the bars of the wrought-iron gate that has protected the basement since an intruder kicked in its steel door—must be on vacation.

When my ex-husband and I moved here, there were two doorbells, one per floor, under mailboxes in the vestibule between the unlocked entry door and the locked interior door. Those became useless when, after a thief jimmied the interior, the entry was dead-bolted.

Not wanting to pay an electrician to move the wiring, we bought wireless ones, which worked, at best, intermittently. As a result, guests were, in those pre-cellphone days, forced to announce their arrival by banging on the door until we heard and, maybe, let them in.

When, post-divorce, the house became all mine, the lack of a doorbell suited me just fine. In time, my habit of ignoring knocks brought on a shutting off: Jehovah's Witnesses skipped my house, neighbors forgot about me, "in your neighborhood" drop-ins ceased.

What about people who didn't give up easily? Who knocked and knocked? Simple: I waited them out. Then, carefully so as not to reveal any sign of life in the house, I'd tiptoe over and peek through the peephole to make sure the knocker was gone for good.

Delivery people were confused: "A house with no doorbell?" Friends were puzzled: "Why don't you have a doorbell?" Family pointed out, as if I hadn't noticed: "You don't have a doorbell." I made noises about having it fixed *soon* but never followed through.

Why be so stubborn about this? After all, I'd had a long, and successful, history of bending over backwards to do things the *right* way—i.e., how others believed things should be done—in order to fit in. Thus, to most eyes, nothing about me seemed *wrong*.

Why risk *normal* for a stupid doorbell—the lack of which might make people take a closer look? Why risk being labeled *quirky, reclusive,* or, worse, *plain crazy?* Why risk raised eyebrows turning into whispers that I was hiding some terrible secret in my home?

Which I was: things inside—e.g., dearth of human foods in fridge, rain pouring through porch roof, twenty-plus cats—were *wrong*. And how panic-stricken I felt when someone came into my home, as if *every* other wanted to, and could, take over me? *Very wrong.*

Like the dogged knockers mentioned earlier. Only after they left did I stop stifling my breath and scrunching my body. Only then dare to turn on TV, lamp, or dryer. Only then open or close a window. Only then was my home mine again. Only then was I truly safe.

When John came into my life, he didn't make a big deal out of the doorbell. Even after moving in, he never insisted that our lives would be *better* in some way if I changed my mind. Which I didn't about that but did, after a while, about inviting family, friends, and,

yes, when necessary, strangers, into our home. We still don't have a doorbell. Almost everybody mentions it but now I can shrug off those jabs without offering a pretense. There is a downside: missed deliveries now and then . . . the very reason I'm in this post

office where the clerk, who has seen me many times, takes my driver's license. His eyes dart: face, ID, slip, ID. When he's certain that I am who I'm claiming to be, he hands over the package, which, by the way, has NO DOORBELL scrawled across my name.

We Take Down a Wall

When John asks, "Do you want to take down a wall?"
I know the one he means:
it encloses the newly discovered fireplace in the first-floor kitchen.
Thirty-five years of living here and I never thought twice about *behind* the wall
       until my sister-in-law called it *blind*.
When my knuckles knocked, a hollow reply told the truth.

John traces lines to guide the saw.
He doesn't cut the frame of two-by-fours.
What's behind is unbroken, ordinary yet strange:
brick hearth, concrete lintel, both once painted high-gloss white that has yellowed.
Even with the wall gone, the space clings to its tomb-silence; maybe it's been closed off
       for too many years?

I reach into, across, the hearth then press palm on stone no one, within memory,
       has touched.
What hung from the nails, which, when pried out, left pocks?
Why does slightly rusted tin cover the flue?
Why aren't base bricks as neatly finished?
On the jamb, white pushes against, but doesn't take over, an odd patch of grey;
       what protected the grey?

At first glance I know:
This fireplace wasn't where families posed for holiday snapshots.
Agents never praised it as "boosting the house's sale appeal."
No, day and night, without ado, it did its working-class job:
held the stove within its surround, spread warmth through uninsulated rooms,
       kept the house from going up in flames.

Rather than demolish and erase, whoever built the wall did a quick-and-dirty cover-up.
For which I give thanks.
After hours of work, the fireplace has been returned to our sight;
we'll have to figure out how to use it from now on.
For the meantime, the wood frame, though no longer needed, will stay in place.

How It Happened, Part 4

We replace the windows, which had never fit.
We install an alarm system and better locks.

When I meet John, he doesn't even try to kiss me for a few dates, which makes me sure
he won't stick around because something's *wrong* with me. But he doesn't leave. In fact,
when he realizes, from the absence of food in the fridge, I don't eat much or well, he
buys groceries and fixes sit-down meals. Months pass before I see: we're building a life.

We rip out the worn stairs but save the elegant handrail and post.
We enlarge rooms by taking down false ceilings.

Though I'm happier and *safer* than I've ever been, panic attacks wreck my sleep. I decide
to see a new therapist. For many hours I say what I think she wants to hear because if I
please her then she'll like me and will tell me *exactly* what I should and shouldn't do. I'll
be fixed, quickly and for life. But she wants me to please me; that ends up taking years.

We paint the kitchen Van Gogh yellow.
We upgrade wiring on the second floor, then the first.

I sign up for a poetry workshop. Week after week the teacher pushes, *hide less, go
further, get out of your head*. I, greedy for praise, complain to John, *She hates my poems
and me*. Yet something inside knows better. I keep going. My poems change bit by bit—
become less about clever and surface; become more about life, more about underneath.

We strip and refinish hardwood floors.
We plant rosemary, which flourishes in our full-sun yard.

Years after our first meeting at Frost Place, Jack becomes my best friend. We talk about
poetry all the time though we don't talk about poetry much. Instead we wander through
Greenmarket on Saturday mornings; drink vinho verde while Johanna and her friends,
glammed in sequins, lip-sync on the roof; laugh so hard at life we nearly pee in our pants.

My Crooked House

The Two-Thirty in the Morning List

Not taking care of haven't made appointment with missed another chance to wasting too much time on Not taking care of keep coming up against not doing enough for should have kept mouth shut about Not taking care of letting get away with haven't given answer to spent too much money on Not taking care of this or that or him or her or me

7. Atomic Time

I want to show my new therapist what a "good" client I am, so, after reading that early or late are signs of resistance, which, in my eyes, means "bad," I arrive on the dot for every session. This isn't as easy to do as it sounds because my watch, a gift from John, doesn't have minute lines, which leaves me uncertain—2:28 or 2:29? I count on my cellphone because the phone company sets its network by NIST-F1, a cesium atomic clock, which won't gain or lose a second in 100 million years. But after all the time spent on having perfect timing, such a letdown: no gold star, no hint I'm her favorite. In fact, now and then she runs a few minutes late. How dare she? She must know how "bad" that is, right?

Fitted Sheets

At the age of fifty-six, I don't know how to fold a fitted sheet. Even worse, I feel folding fitted sheets into small neat rectangles that fit on shelves in an orderly fashion is beyond my abilities. I am not kidding. Every week when the sheets come out of the dryer I start folding with optimism—this time I will surely figure it out—and end with rumpled messes, which spill onto the floor when anyone opens the linen closet door. Every week my belief becomes stronger: I am broken in some fundamental way and thus incapable of learning how to fold a fitted sheet. I trust my ability to understand complex scientific theories such as dark matter or to fix an outage affecting sixty-thousand telephone lines or to travel alone in a foreign country but not my competency with easily-mastered-by-everyone-else-in-the-universe tasks such as applying makeup, buying shoes that fit, blow-drying my hair, managing money, cooking simple meals, housekeeping, or tending a flower garden. It has been this way my whole life. Sure I get by because you can get by with wrinkled sheets in disorderly closets by pretending you're above worrying about such nonsense but, truth be told, week after week I'm in the basement trying to figure it out.

Annotated Map of Panic Attacks, Location E

F. M. Kirby Shakespeare Theater, seat 106, middle of row K.
Saturday matinee of *The Comedy of Errors*. The house lights haven't gone down, yet I'm already worrying about when the attack will hit because for years I haven't made it through a play without one. The ritual checking of left and right: picking best escape route. Although it's never happened, my frantic exit loops in my head: me clambering over people, them snarling. But today when, during Act One, the falling-backwards-feeling violates my mind, I grab John's hand—the signal set when I, not long ago, let him in on my secret. His hand envelops mine. For the first time in my life, an attack retreats.

Homemaking, Part I

House Ghosts

#1

This first floor hallway door hasn't opened to the world in fifty years. Its pitted interior face remains to be seen. Its exterior long buried. No trace of steps that once connected sill to street. Steeple-tipped hinges painted shut. A single nail—through keyhole into board—prevents right-hand swing. The transom, layered with staid colors, no longer lets in light.

#2

Because of faulty depth perception, my eyes can't find it without my hands: this door-case-shaped bump that unsettles a weight-bearing wall. A century ago, guests stepped through, into the parlor—nowadays my studio. How long has the space defined by it been trapped between sheetrock? How long since someone used it to cross from there to here?

#3

"Your house almost burned down," says my neighbor, who, since her birth in 1923, has lived in a house that borders our yard. Nothing supports her claim until siding is ripped off: around one window, a charred burst, as if glass-shattering flames yearned for us to remember how close a fight it was. Ah, but the damaged wood didn't need to be replaced.

#4

On this certificate, dated February 9, 1949, issued to the owner of this house, allowing him to switch from coal to oil, red print: *Keep this certificate in boiler/furnace room*. The Department of Smoke Regulation has been gone for decades yet this paper's kept on a beam. Funny how words that have lost the power to harm can be given the power to rule.

#5

The first step in reclaiming our backyard: remediating the dirt. The first step in remediating dirt: dig deep. As we dig, we pick out small, unwanted rocks. Near the fence the spade hits pieces too big for hands: bluestones from a foundation. Another story proves true: this ground was strong enough to bear the vibration of lace-making looms.

#6

The porch roof leaks unseen until chunks of plaster fall. Things quickly go from bad to worse: any storm means buckets and mops. No matter how much I patch, rain pours in. When the ruined walls are stripped to their bones, rough-sawn shiplap marks only one as original to the house. No wonder there were problems: this room a poorly built add-on.

#7

One door on the cramped upper landing leads into our kitchen. The other leads into the wall-length closet in what's now the dining room. This door and the space beyond puzzle me until a friend paces out the floor plan before a one-family house was split into two: the out-of -place door cuts us off from a hallway that linked what were then all bedrooms.

#8

The author of a nineteenth-century history of West Hoboken, which was what this section of Union City was called back then, rhapsodizes about "many a happy hour spent" where wildflowers grew, rabbits and birds abounded, in a woods of cedar trees that included our 4,421 square feet. Somewhere, still, deep beneath the foundation, the old woodland lasts.

To My House

Nobody else, I think
while roaming your top floor
in darkness, *can do this.*
Nobody else, I think
while up and down your flight
in darkness, *can do this.*
Nobody else, I think
while roaming your first floor
in darkness, *can do this.*
I know you well enough
to walk around what's solid.
I know you well enough
to walk into what's shadow.
House, I know you like a book.

Gone

for Jack Wiler

Three days before, we give a reading at the Main Street Museum in White River Junction. As always you blow off the roof with your performance. You also do a great job reading the Talker role in one of my sideshow poems. The audience loves you. Afterwards our host takes us to dinner at a fancy place, not a chain or a dive. She tells us to order whatever we want from the menu and whatever we want from the bar. We drink glass after glass of a good merlot; eat scallops and filet mignon; laugh at everyone's stories about the poetry world. At one point you, a satisfied calm on your face, turn to me and say, "This is the first time I really feel like I'm being treated with respect as a poet."

Two days before, we eat breakfast at the Polka Dot Diner and you ask if I really told you that *We Monsters* wasn't the right title for your next collection or if you dreamed the conversation. When I answer that you dreamed it, you tell me that you're thinking of changing the title but don't know to what. We drive from Vermont to New Jersey in a terrible storm. You're in the back seat. You complain about a chill. At various times during the trip I hear mumbling and turn to see if you're talking to John or me. I'm a little worried because you seem to be pleading in a childlike way with an invisible person. When we drop you off, I give you a hug and say, "I love reading with you." You agree.

Thirty hours before, I send that new poem for your comment but you don't answer. Fifteen minutes before, I'm walking towards the car because John and I are going to Tuesday night yoga when he comes out of the garage, his eyes full of shock, and says, "Johanna just called. Jack's gone." Gone where? Oh no, did they have another big fight and Jack walked out? Gone where? And John looks at me and keeps saying, "He's gone." One minute before, I'm walking down the hallway to your bedroom and telling the cops standing outside the door that we're close friends and I haven't yet stepped into the room, haven't yet seen your body, covered with a sheet, on the floor, haven't yet seen your face.

And then there's only before.

October Night, 2009

for Jack Wiler

I dreamt fixed stars, while overhead
Orion slid from East to West.

Before the light erased his form
I woke and caught last glimpse.

                             Yet what

seemed true by eye, proved false by heart:
though now unseen, he's never gone.

The Unexpected Visit

Last night, while we were sleeping, Death stopped by for Helen—one of two cats left downstairs. We weren't expecting it. She'd showed no signs of being sick until she collapsed in the middle of the cold kitchen floor and didn't get up—not even to pee.

She wasn't a favorite of mine. By the time a twist of fate dropped her in my lap, I didn't want to take in another stray—certainly not a nearly dead kitten with such a bad infection that both eyes had to be removed. More visits to the vet, more bills, more of less for me.

I woke with a start. Death was slipping into our home, gliding through the hall. John's warmth filled the space to my left. Bart purred against my legs. I held my breath for the three of us. "Please," I begged (the way that, as a child, I did while hiding in the closet):

"Don't find us. Don't take John. Don't take Bart who's shrunk to skin and bones from a tumor. Let him stay longer—a week, half a day. Let me wake in the morning with this same life, the life that I was always waiting for, intact. Oh, Death, don't come upstairs."

What I Was Waiting For

John says, before he falls asleep each night,
without a hint of dark, "I love you, Tree."
Some nights, awake enough, I add my part,
"And I love you, the sun, the moon, the stars."
Yet even when I'm too far gone to speak,
to hear, and words get missed, his love, his love, abides.

About Time through Time, Parts 8 and 9

8. It Is Time

The *best* mornings are the ones
when I take my coffee back to bed,
where John and Bart are still sleeping,
and listen to their sounds, feel their warmth, smell their smells.
This morning is a *best* morning,
except Bart is near death—so frail he can no longer jump;
we tenderly pick him up, tenderly place him between us.
He has been fading away for weeks, but I see now, now it is time.

9. 3:31 A.M.

My mind flooded with unfinished work:
the clunky word in a poem, the mountain of dirty laundry,
the unreturned phone call to a dear friend, last month's invoice,
an apology to John for the mistake I made that cost us the trick in bridge.
The clock face tells me, "Go back to sleep."
My mind stops me; I don't understand why until,
at last crossing the edge of sleep, a nether voice spells it out:
I must let go of time.

The Power of the Novena

At almost every family gathering, we end up having one of those debates
lapsed Catholics seem fond of.
Tonight's topic: *Do novenas work?* I confess:
my petition for *all* As was answered; *make Mousey love me* was not.
Annie jumps in with "No" because she was never given drawing lessons.
A second "No" from Louise, whose birthday we're here to celebrate,
who wore down the white plastic beads of her First Communion rosary praying for a bike
never received. Joanie doesn't take a side.
But Johnny (who's been chewing off Tommy's ear with a funny riff
about how he feigned stomachaches to dodge
nine nights in a row of endless recitations of *Hail, Mary, full of grace* . . .
led by Mom from her rocking chair, us on our knees)
suddenly stands, drops the laughter from his voice, and sums things up,
"Look, those novenas did work: you and you and you and you and you and I survived."

My Crooked House

John wants to put a metal frame around our house as a way of correcting its lean.

He already put metal beams under the floor in the first-floor kitchen in an attempt to reverse its sagging.

He points out how the straight edge of the new built-in bookcase in the first-floor living room calls attention to the ceiling slant.

The space between wall and frame of the back door changes from 2¾ inches at the base to 4¼ inches at the top.

The second floor has its own set of problems: much carpentry had to be done to the kitchen window to square it on the wall, and objects that fall on the dining-room floor roll from north to south.

This morning he, while sitting in the yard, noticed how the stairs are off-center from the door.

"Yes," I say to him, "all over there are signs of the leans, slants, settles, sags, and cracks underneath."

"But," I add, "this house has survived a century; it does not need to be straightened out."

Homemaking, Part II

Concussion (continued)

Minutes before, we're leaving a reading in Bryant Park.
I'm laughing because, minutes before, when someone says, "Looks like rain,"
I say, "No, the skies have been threatening all day without a drop,"
then, minutes before, a drizzle starts—
though there's no wind to speak of
at that time.
Minutes before, we're hurrying to catch the 8:40 bus.
Minutes before, I fall two steps behind because John's walking too fast.
Minutes before, a gust down 41st turns umbrella into missile, which, one minute before,
before I see, deals dead-on blow to face.
Skull slams on slate.
The *CRACK* swallows me whole,
undoes my minutes.
The narrative takes a turn.

For once in my life I stay on the ground,
don't downplay what's happened
by waving it off with "Really, I'm fine,"
or jokes about hard Lamphier heads.
For once in my life the routine flight—
MUST don't let RUN them see
HIDE you're hurting NOW—
is replaced by a newborn form of fight.
For once in my life John's kneeling at my side,
paying 100 percent attention,
telling the truth about what's going on,
watching, but not taking, over.
For once in my life I know in my heart of hearts
the person I love, loves me.

for Jack Wiler

You said that angels appeared around your bed when you were near death,
that they helped you make it through the night, then and from then on.
You insisted they were real, not hallucinations from fevers.
I, who many times begged, to no avail, angels for help,
who'd never say so because you were my friend,
didn't believe your story
because I no longer believed in them.

Still, as fear rushed in, cutting me off
from me, from John, they
appeared. Some built a roof with a subway map,
a pizza box, their bodies, and the very umbrella that had
knocked me down. One kept calling 911. One slid his t-shirt
under my head. And you, you were there, in a beat, urging me, as always:
"Pay attention." When I did, fear backed down, leaving me free to get through.

As we wait for help to come,
John never drops my hand.

And though we don't say much,
I'm sure, to my surprise,
there's nothing left unsaid.

But more surprising still:
at what may be my end,
instead of *not enough*,

I'm filled with *satisfied*—
with now, with us, with me.

What's your name?	Answered quickly.
Date of birth? And today?	Answered both quickly.
Home address?	Answered quickly.
Who's the president?	This one stumped me for a few seconds.
Where are you?	Answered quickly.
What happened?	Answered quickly.
Any vomiting?	No.
The pain on a scale of 1 to 10?	Fought urge to answer 1. Answered 8.
~~The fear on a scale of 1 to 10?~~	~~Not asked.~~
Did you pass out?	No.
Do you feel this? This? This? This?	A squeeze of every hand and foot.
Why are you holding up her legs?	This question wasn't directed at me.
Can you make it on your own?	Tried but wasn't steady.
Is someone with you?	Yes.

From the get-go, my oldest habit kicks in: neither my body nor my mind will trust a soul. Regardless how much I've pretended to let others take care of me at various times in my life, I've always been secretly working out what to do when the inevitable abandonment happened—even if it only happened in my head. Except now I'm in over my head. Now, even if I were able to make a plan, I'm incapable of executing one. Now I must trust that, if necessary, John knows who I am, what I want and wouldn't want. I can do this. Now I must trust EMTs, which means forgetting about trying to please them, about staying quiet so as not to appear too needy. I can do this. Then the heart of the habit must be dealt with: mind doesn't really trust body—especially when it's uncontrollably shaking as it is right now. In truth, mind has always found body's needs—e.g., food, sleep, the touch of another—disgusting, and turned a deaf ear to its cries for more than the least. Body rose up now and again but mind used shame to crush those rebellions. Except, in this situation, even stubborn mind sees that body knows best what to do, that any chance I have of surviving depends on its skills. Mind steps out of the way, lets body take over the show.

Turns out my friends aren't so far away—at the Grill, on the opposite side of the park.
They have no clue about my fall.
That's how it goes, doesn't it?
Connected, but not.
The second we're out of each other's sight, who knows what happens?
One by one, I'll tell them a form of the night.
They'll be struck by the randomness of it all.
They'll tiptoe around the undetected clots that may take me down, down the line.
But right now, when I can't get to the ambulance under my own power,
they're safe from this storm: sipping a summer drink like a G&T,
shooting the breeze about great and not-so-great readings of their own.
Still, I bet each glances through the glass—maybe on hearing that thunderclap—
makes, as I do, a mental note about the terrible wind and rain,
feels, if only for the briefest point in time, the same strange awe.

Blood pressure checked again, again by EMT:
"unstable" signals swelling or hemorrhage in brain.
Though numbers settle down to "normal range," they may deceive:
the "gold standard" for seeing what is really going on inside,
at least right here, right now: a CT scan.
Siren cuts through jam on 42nd Street.
Tires hit bumps and holes along the way but I don't make a stink—
this white steed carries me away from doubt.

In "fast track" trauma area, the RN palpates "goose egg," dispenses ice pack,
       updates chart,
then doesn't say another word to me.
Stares straight ahead when she walks by.
As if this melting ice were failsafe fix for whatever may be broken in my head.
At no-rhyme-or-reason intervals, the urgent care MD, who never shows his face,
       yells out a name.
As that lucky name proceeds into Exam Room #1, the blank RN, without a hint
       of urgency, runs down the cases left.
I'm always last on list, am always named "woman umbrella hit,"
which sounds as far from real emergency as one can get,
as if I'm making "big fat deal" about a stupid scratch—
"acting like baby of the family," screams inner voice that isn't mine.

Across the room, "sharp stomach pain" paces and sobs.
She CAN'T PUT UP WITH THIS . . . CAN'T . . . WON'T . . . can't . . . please.
The number of patients dwindles to me.
Out of the blue, the RN turns off lights—"fast track" shutting down for night.
Huh? Am I invisible? Maybe they're pointing out:
hours have passed since fall and still no danger signs. Why waste their time?
The MD finally waves me in, checks this and that, says to the chart,
"If you want I'll order a CT scan, though I'm fairly certain everything is fine."

I get it: he wants to leave.

Because of protocol, he must bring up the CT scan but doesn't want to wait around—
could take a while, he warns—for radiology to fit me in.

Part of me jumps to sign the form that'll let him off the hook if "fairly certain" proves
      not right.

Part of me wishes John would take a stand.

But I'm the one—not him or him—who felt that *CRACK*.

So, no; I'll stay as long as it may take

until this MD holds the true "gold standard" in his hands,

until he looks me in the eye and says, "Mrs. Carson, your picture's clear."

Then, and only then, will I go home.

for Anne Fischer

Midway through the next week, I find myself
in Bryant Park; the "goose egg" now a bruise,
plus no new symptoms have appeared, but, well,

the fact that time may be cut short still true—
in which case, official reports will meet
the weight of proof that John will need to sue.

I want to track them down, yet dread to be
with no arm to grip if dizziness hits
in the midst of loud 42nd Street,

since losing balance while ringed by tourists
will spark a panic attack. Aftermath?
Usual shame times ten. A friend submits

to play the guide: she makes a narrow pass
through crowds—providing the comfort of air
and light—slows steps to mimic mine, throws wrath

at heedless drivers, checks my eyes for fear.
Though the way's not hard, deep, savage, or dark,
I'd lose heart, reader, unless she stays near.

To start, we find a worker at the park,
who's heard about my fall, but blanks his face
when quizzed for more. At Midtown South the sergeant

shrugs, "No incident for that night, that place,
put into system yet. Try in a week
or two." This bad news resurrects the ache.

I, out of ideas and drained of strength, freeze
at the thought of returning here. Before
things spiral down too far, my wise guide seeks

Gate 406 where homeward buses board.
We cross the Hudson—via the tunnel
of squeals and fumes—then see again my door.

A year later my doctor reads
the follow-up CT scan and says,
"Everything about your head
appears normal."

Acknowledgments

"The Last Session" includes quotes from: Andrew Jacobs, "NEIGHBORHOOD REPORT: WEST VILLAGE; Mystery Ends But Its Traces Still Remain," New York Times, http://www.nytimes.com/1995/11/12/nyregion/neighborhood-report-west-village-mystery-ends-but-its-traces-still-remain.html.

Some of these poems, or earlier versions of them, have appeared, or are forthcoming, in the following journals:

The Aurorean: "October Night, 2009"
Blue Collar Review: "Workplace Humor"
Edison Literary Review: "Fitted Sheets"
Journal of New Jersey Poets: "The Power of the Novena"
Psychoanalytic Perspectives: "Annotated Map of Panic Attacks," "My Crooked House," "The Last Session," "The Unexpected Visit"

Thanks to:

Playwright Dael Orlandersmith, who helped me to draw the original map.
The friends who gave me encouragement and support along the way: Cat Doty, Dawn Potter, Mary Hennessey, Anne Fischer, Tülây Fatma Ugural, Angela Santillo, Florenz Eisman.
The staff at CavanKerry Press who, as always, did great work: Starr Troup, Donna Rutkowski, Catherine Breitfeller, Greg Smith, Baron Wormser, Dawn Potter.

Special thanks to:

Joan Cusack Handler whose skillful, generous and insightful editing has made this a better book.
My family whose love and support gives me courage: Joan Lamphier, Anne & Peter Cade, Louise Lamphier, John Lamphier & Joan Pollock, Thomas & Sue Lamphier.
Jack Wiler whose spirit fills these poems.
John and Rivka for everything they bring to my life.

CavanKerry's Mission

CavanKerry Press is a not-for-profit literary press dedicated to art and community. From its inception in 2000, its vision has been to present, through poetry and prose, *Lives Brought to Life* and to create programs that bring CavanKerry books and writers to diverse audiences.

Other Books in the LaurelBooks Series